PERFECT
COMPOST

Simon Akeroyd

 National Trust

First published in the United Kingdom in 2020 by
National Trust Books
43 Great Ormond Street
London
WC1N 3HZ

An imprint of Pavilion Books Company Ltd

ISBN 978-1-91135-894-7

A CIP catalogue record for this book is available from the British Library.

10 9 8 7 6 5 4 3 2 1

Reproduction by Rival Colour Ltd, UK
Printed and bound by Toppan Leefung Printing Ltd, China

This book can be ordered direct from the publisher at www.pavilionbooks.com

Illustrations by Abi Read

CONTENTS

INTRODUCTION

This book will encourage you to try composting at home. Not only does homemade compost make a great soil improver, it is also a practical way of managing your kitchen and garden waste.

Despite all the known benefits of gardening, recycling and creating a sustainable planet, according to a 2014 survey conducted by the UK waste management company Business Waste, 97 per cent of the population have never composted or had a compost heap. This is a great shame, particularly as we are a nation of gardeners, with gardening recognised as the nation's number one hobby.

There are a number of possible reasons for this lack of composting among British households, but the main three are as follows. Firstly, people perceive it as hard, time-consuming work. Secondly, they don't think they have enough outdoor space. And thirdly, they think it requires skills that they don't possess.

Additionally, very often composting is seen as one of the dark arts: an esoteric, magical process, as plant and kitchen waste is transformed into gardening 'gold' that only the horticultural equivalent of an alchemist is capable of achieving. It is often seen as beyond the skills and realm of the average person to produce good compost in the garden.

This book aims to debunk these myths, and to show that creating compost doesn't have to be hard work or time-consuming, hardly requires any space, and is actually relatively easy. Whether you have a tiny courtyard garden or a huge country estate, there is almost always enough room for composting. Compact, modern compost bin designs mean they can be squeezed into the tiniest of spaces. In addition, using contemporary, sometimes beautifully coloured materials for your compost facilities can look chic and fashionable and help you to show off your 'green' environmental credentials to your neighbours.

This book is divided into three chapters. In the first chapter, we outline why it is a good idea to make compost at home. Reasons for this include reducing our environmental impact on the planet, saving time and money, and improving growing conditions in the garden. In the second chapter, we explore the different types of composting facilities you can install in your garden, ranging from large composting bays made from recycled pallets to compact, labour-saving types that can be rotated simply by turning a handle. In the third and final chapter we cover how to make compost, including the science behind the art and a list of the top 10 tips on how to create perfect compost.

Compost-making is very rewarding and you're doing something great for the environment, but, most of all, it is fun, and it's definitely worth giving it a try.

WHY COMPOST?

SPREADING
THE MESSAGE

Growing plants is good for the environment and yet, despite a general increase in gardening over the last few decades, green spaces are being lost all the time to property and land developers. In urban areas, owners are covering over gardens with concrete, block paving and patios, especially front gardens, which are often converted into driveways and parking spaces. This is damaging to the environment as it leads to a dramatic reduction in wildlife habitats and biodiversity, as well as a loss of garden plants, including the trees and shrubs that absorb excess carbon and pollution from the atmosphere and pump out clean oxygen for us to breathe.

Almost as importantly, fewer plants in urban settings, coupled with more gardens covered with these impermeable surfaces, will dramatically exacerbate the problem of 'run-off' during the increasing rainfall we are currently experiencing, inevitably leading to increased incidence of flooding.

Adding compost to your front garden and keeping your personal space green and full of life rather than turning it into a parking space will reduce considerably the likelihood of flash flooding, since the organic material not only improves drainage but naturally absorbs water like a sponge, gradually releasing it as and when plants require it. Because of this, it is more important than ever that people are encouraged to make their own compost and use it to grow better plants, which in turn may well inspire

Adding homemade compost to a front garden can create a lush, wildlife-friendly space, looks more attractive than a driveway, and is better for the environment.

other people to create gardens, to value green spaces and to reverse this trend of rapid decline in urban and city environments. A gorgeous front garden, packed full of healthy plants because they are growing in lovely homemade compost, is a wonderful advertisement to encourage others to grow plants, reuse their own green waste and create a greener planet.

COMPOSTING ISN'T
A DIRTY WORD

The compost area is the engine room of the garden. A garden's sustainability and environmental credentials are definitively improved by recycling garden waste.

Sadly, in the past, many garden designers have treated composting as almost an afterthought, once all the niceties of designing and planting a garden have been done. Yet an effective and efficient compost site is probably the single most important aspect of managing a garden. It should possibly be at the forefront of every garden designer's thinking process to create a living, breathing ecosystem, with any design based first and foremost around a sustainable compost site. And perhaps not tucked away around the back of the garden either, hidden away as a shameful secret. Thankfully, attitudes are changing. Great gardeners are great composters, and the two skills go hand in hand. Modern gardeners are often proud of their composting credentials and can make the compost heap a key feature in their garden.

Love your compost

Beauty is often said to be in the eye of the beholder, and for many modern gardeners composting is regarded as a thing of beauty. The smell of a well-decomposed compost heap has a gentle, sweet scent, albeit slightly earthy, that is as natural and enjoyable as that of many garden plants. At the same time, running your fingers through its friable texture can quicken the pulse as you think about the potential plants that can be grown in this naturally created substance. A well-turned compost comes in a range of rich shades, varying from dark chocolaty depths to intense light or almost golden hues which would give any designer trying to select dark brown or black planting schemes a run for their money. Modern composting facilities can also look cool, modern and chic, are bang on trend, and make a great talking point in any garden.

SAVE MONEY WHILE SAVING THE PLANET

Probably the biggest incentive for households to start composting is that it can save you money. Millions of pounds a year are spent by people buying bags of compost from garden centres. Readymade compost is expensive, especially when used as a soil improver, yet you can make your own compost for free at home. Furthermore, you don't even have to expend the fuel or time driving to the garden centre to collect some. Home composting is simply transforming the kitchen and garden waste that you're already generating into something worth its weight in gold as far as the health of your plants, the soil and the planet are concerned. And it costs absolutely nothing. And also ...

Composting your garden waste at home saves countless trips to the reycling centre.

... it saves trips to the tip

It is possible to rack up mileage and fuel bills by driving back and forth to your local recycling site with your car laden full with garden waste. Not only does it cost a fortune in petrol, but all those fumes are damaging for the planet. An average-sized garden will produce about a tonne of garden waste per year, and many will produce far more. If everybody in the neighbourhood drives their garden waste to be recycled it creates an enormous carbon footprint. The environmental and ecological impact is huge. In addition, it is time-consuming for individuals to queue up at recycling centres with hundreds of other neighbours to drop off their garden waste. If people were to compost their material at home instead, the planet would be far more sustainable. In addition, who wouldn't prefer relaxing in their garden admiring their happy, healthy plants to sitting in their car in a queue of traffic? And of course, you'd avoid making a mess of your car boot and back seats each time it is laden full of green waste. Not to mention the twigs you find weeks later in odd and painful places, and the bugs and insects hiding in your car that should have remained in your garden.

It's good for the environment

About 15 million tonnes of household food waste are wasted each year in Britain. Although many councils provide food waste collection, and in some places, free (or low-cost) garden waste collection, there are of course huge bulk transport costs and a number of associated environmental impacts with this system of waste management. It is far better for the environment to compost as much of your kitchen waste at home as you can.

Very often bought composts are pumped full of slow- or controlled-release synthetic fertilisers and many of them contain peat, extracted from environmentally sensitive and fragile ecosystems. This isn't a sustainable method of horticulture. Making your own compost at home ensures you know exactly what has gone into it. It is made by you, adding your own ingredients from food or plants you have grown at home. Unlike bought compost it will not be wrapped in single-use plastic, which itself usually has to go off to landfill once you have emptied it, nor are there any carbon and pollutant emissions associated with transporting it. Unless you have a diesel-powered wheelbarrow, of course.

The environmental benefits for making your own compost go even further. Because it doesn't break down efficiently, when garden and food waste goes into landfill, it produces large amounts of methane. This type of greenhouse gas is a major contributor to damaging the ozone layer, and increases global warming. If everybody was to compost at home, this would dramatically reduce the damage caused by methane.

THE JOY OF
COMPOSTING

It is well recognised that gardening is good for the planet, as well as for your physical and mental health.

Turning over your compost can be great exercise, yet, for people with disabilities or an aversion to enjoying the physicality, there are composting systems that involve next to no work. For example, rotating compost bins are available for which you simply turn a handle that spins the drums for you. Whether you choose this method or turn it over yourself, composting will encourage you outdoors and into the fresh air.

Once you have a supply of free homemade compost, the next natural and healthy step is to use it, even if it is just to plant up a container or the hanging basket by your front door. Plants are good for the planet, and provide the oxygen we breathe, as well as mopping up excessive carbon dioxide in the atmosphere. Creating your own compost will encourage you to grow more and will be one more step in helping out the planet.

Benefits for your garden

By adding homemade garden compost to the soil, you are reducing the need to use water, a valuable and costly resource, as compost's high humus content helps to retain moisture. You'll also find you have less of a need for artificial fertilisers and chemicals, which are produced synthetically in factories and flown all over the world, racking up air miles, in order to distribute them from garden centres or online so that they may be used in gardens. It's far better for the environment to use homemade garden compost, which will often contain enough nutrients for most plants to grow in.

Incorporating garden compost into the soil increases the strength of a plant, giving it a healthy environment to grow in. A healthy plant will be far more robust than a sickly, weak one, and much less likely to succumb to pests and diseases. This increased resistance in turn reduces the need to use chemical insecticides and fungicides.

Beneficial bacteria and fungi flourish far more readily in garden compost and soil enriched with compost than in poor, barren, infertile soil. The entirely natural ecosystem will encourage a healthier plant environment, attracting beneficial organisms both above and beneath the soil, and making a far more sustainable garden.

Applying homemade compost to the garden prevents soil erosion by encouraging plants to develop strong root systems that hold soil structures together, preventing it from washing away. Compost also encourages strong growth above ground, which shelters and protects the ground beneath it from desiccating winds. In the garden itself, compost fortifies turf against wear and tear on the lawn, and holds flower beds in place that could otherwise collapse or wash away in heavy rains.

Benefits for your health

It is thought that fruit and veg grown in natural, homemade compost contain more nutrients and are healthier to eat than crops grown using artificial fertilisers or in infertile soil. After all, a plant's nutrients are a direct consequence of the soil the roots are growing in. And of course, the soil will potentially have had no chemicals used on it, as the beneficial garden environment will have encouraged natural predators and the plants would have had better resistance to pests and diseases.

Use homemade compost to mulch around plants: it will retain moisture and suppress weeds.

MAKING FREE MULCH FOR YOUR GARDEN

Mulch is any material that gardeners place over the soil to help retain moisture and suppress weeds. There are inorganic materials that can be used, such as pebbles, slates, shells or landscape membrane, but one of the best types of mulch is the free garden compost that you've made yourself. Although its nutrient content might be a little variable, the organic, natural material you have made improves the soil's structure, increases the drainage of clay soils and adds bulk to light, thin, sandy soils. Exposed soil is also prone to erosion, and mulching with well-rotted compost will prevent it from deteriorating further. It is of course possible to buy composted mulch, but this can be extremely expensive, especially if you have a large area to cover. It is far cheaper and more sustainable to make your own lovely compost to spread onto your flower beds.

Garden compost mulch can be coarser than the kind of compost you use for seed-sowing or potting up plants, but the mix of smaller and larger pieces will open up your soil, whatever its type.

Some gardeners dig the material in straight away, while others who prefer a no-dig approach leave it on the surface and let the rain and the worms pull it down gradually into the soil, until the soil needs topping up and replenishing with more mulch.

Mulching the beds is also an effective method of returning to the soil the valuable nutrients and other organic materials that have been taken away when tidying up your garden or harvesting your produce. As the mulch decomposes and works its way into the existing soil, it will improve the soil conditions, enriching it with organic matter.

Spreading garden compost as a mulch over existing soil helps to retain moisture in the ground, slowing up the evaporation process and preventing moisture from disappearing too fast. This enables plants to withstand droughts for longer. The additional moisture also helps plants establish a strong, healthy root system and become more robust at dealing with fluctuations in the weather.

Mulching is also effective for suppressing annual weeds that may germinate in exposed, uncovered soil. Covering the soil with garden compost will keep weed seeds in the dark and away from the sunlight they require for germination.

For this to be effective it is important to ensure that the compost itself has got hot enough during the decomposition process to kill off any potential weed seeds or perennial roots. Otherwise these will germinate in your flower beds.

Prior to any mulching activity plants should always be watered, as the mulch will then help contain moisture levels under the material. It's also worth checking that the soil is free from any remaining perennial weeds as these will spread quickly in the richer, moister environment. If your garden compost is very lumpy or still has large pieces of uncomposted material in it, like twigs and wood, you can use a coarse sieve to remove them, adding larger organic material back into the existing compost heap to continue breaking down.

How to mulch

Spread the compost over exposed areas of the existing soil on the flower bed to a depth of 7.5cm (3in). Use a rake to get it as level as possible. Avoid the material coming into direct contact with the plants as it can cause it to rot.

Quick mulch technique

One quick and effective method of mulching a flower bed that has just been planted with smallish plants is to place their flower pots upside down over individual plants before spreading the compost over the beds. Remove the pots and the compost should be nicely away from direct contact with the plants.

Mulch for acidic plants

If you grow acidic soil-loving plants in your garden (often known as ericaceous plants), such as rhododendrons, heathers, azaleas, most magnolias, blueberries and camellias, then you will need to find out whether the compost you are applying to the soil as a mulch isn't too alkaline. A simple pH soil-testing kit can be used to check. If the pH is higher than 5.5 then it should be avoided, and instead an 'acidic' mulch can be applied. The best type of 'acidic' mulch is simply made from pure, rotted pine needles that can be placed over the soil and around the bases of acidic-soil-loving trees and shrubs. Other materials that will slightly 'acidify' compost and can be mixed into neutral compost mulches include rotted oak leaves, coffee granules, decomposed onions and citrus peelings.

Wood chippings

One very effective material for mulching over garden beds to suppress weeds and retain moisture is wood chippings. If you have woody plants in your garden such as trees and shrubs, then using a power tool called a wood chipper is the most effective method of producing your own free source of this invaluable mulch. There are lots of models available, in a range of prices to suit most people's budgets. For smaller branches and leaves a shredder can be used to chop them up into small pieces instead of a chipper. A shredder is very similar to a chipper but uses flails to smash up the material instead of chopping it up with blades. The size of the branch you can chip or shred will depend on the model of chipper you have.

Shredders are useful for breaking up small branches, twigs or wood material to add to the compost heap.

Chippers and shredders are brilliant for recycling garden material such as branches and other woody material that may otherwise be too bulky to take to the local recycling centre. Always wear protective clothing such as eye protection and gloves when operating one. For very large branches it may be worth paying a professional to chip the material for you.

Wood chip should be spread over the surface of flower beds and around trees and shrubs to a depth of between 5 and 10cm (2–4in). As with spreading garden compost, ensure that wood chippings avoid direct contact with trunks and foliage as this can cause the plant to rot.

Fresh wood chippings can deplete the soil of nitrogen, a key nutrient required for plant growth. Fresh material can also 'burn' the roots as the material breaks down. It is therefore recommended that wood chippings are left for three to four months to decompose before using them as a mulch in the garden. The best way to store them is in a heap, occasionally turned to speed up their decomposition. Once the material is beginning to rot it is ready to use in the garden.

Wood chippings can also be added to standard compost heaps too, as they are carbon-rich and help break down nitrogen-rich material such as grass clippings or kitchen waste.

Instead of chipping or shredding twigs and branches, large woody material, including trunks, can be left in areas of the garden to rot down as wood piles which will encourage a range of wildlife.

Autumn leaves can be converted into leaf mould, a useful material for mulching or using in potting compost.

MAKING YOUR OWN FREE LEAF MOULD

A shredder can also be used to make leaf mould, which is another effective material for using as a mulch on flower beds. Fallen leaves in autumn can be annoying when they're strewn across your lawn, flower beds and driveway as they look messy and smother your plants and lawns, sometimes killing anything that becomes covered in a dense carpet. Raking them up or using a leaf blower, and then bagging them up and taking them away, can become a real chore. However, this negative activity can be transformed into a wonderful positive, as fallen leaves make a superb type of compost called leaf mould. It is used as a soil improver and sometimes as a potting compost. It is often low in nutrients, but adds to the friability and structure of the soil. Leaf mould from the garden centre is very expensive, but from your own garden, it is free. See page 84 for more information on making leaf mould.

MAKING YOUR OWN
SEED AND POTTING
COMPOST

On its own, homemade compost is too rich and coarse for growing seeds and young plants, and may contain plant diseases if you are unlucky. It can, however, be sieved finely and combined with ingredients like leaf mould, garden soil, sharp sand or other additives that help with drainage and water retention, to create your own perfect compost recipe. Before using it you may wish to sterilise the mixture in the oven or microwave to prevent any potential pathogen problems.

Top tips for making your own potting and sowing compost:
- Keep your compost consistent, uniform and free of lumps.
- Ensure your compost retains moisture but is free-draining.
- You should aim for plenty of air in the compost, but ensure it is firm enough for roots to grow in.
- Make sure it is free from pests, disease and weeds.
- Match the plant's needs to the compost – for instance, some plants require more nutrients and more drainage than others.

The easiest way to mix your own compost is in a wheelbarrow or on a board. Use a shovel to mix the 'ingredients' together thoroughly, and then store it somewhere dry, such as in a clean dustbin with a lid, until you're ready to use it.

Individual plant requirements vary as to nutrient and drainage levels in soil and compost, but here are some suggested ratios:

HOMEMADE SEED-SOWING MIX

One part

garden soil

One part

leaf mould,
composted bark
or coir

One part

sharp sand

HOMEMADE POTTING-ON MIX

(once seedlings are established)

One part

garden soil

One part

leaf mould

One part

homemade
compost

HOMEMADE POTTING COMPOST MIX FOR LARGE CONTAINERS

One part

garden soil

One part

homemade compost

MAKING YOUR OWN TOP DRESSING FOR LAWNS

If you love your lawn, and want it to look green and healthy, it will benefit from a top dressing using your garden compost. Top dressing is usually mixed in equal ratios using sharp sand, free-draining garden soil and garden compost.

Sieve the top dressing to remove any lumps before using it. Make holes in the lawn by pushing the tines of a garden fork about 5cm (2in) into the surface, at spacings of between 5 and 10cm (2–4in). Use a shovel to spread the top dressing over the lawn, giving the grass a light covering, around 1cm (½in) in depth. Then use a garden besom or stiff-bristled garden brush to sweep the top dressing into the holes so that it is no longer on the surface. This is usually done in autumn, although very keen lawn-lovers will do it a few times throughout the year.

Levelling a lawn with homemade top dressing

Homemade compost can also be used for levelling out the lawn. Over time, lawns can develop dips and hollows as the soil naturally moves underneath, expanding and contracting depending on the weather. Wear and tear from humans can also affect lawn levels, as can digging and tunnelling animals and spreading roots.

To level out a dip in the lawn, use a half-moon tool or spade to cut a cross shape across the hollow at about 4cm (1½in) deep. Fold back the turf flaps to reveal the soil underneath. Loosen the soil with a fork and then use the top dressing mix described above. Tread it down with your garden boots and then fold back the turf flaps and firm them down. Brush more of the top dressing into the cracks between the flaps with a besom, and lightly firm it down.

STERILISING SOIL

Shop-bought compost for seed-sowing and potting is typically sterilised during production to kill off weed seeds and any pathogens that might be present. This process also, of course, kills off any beneficial micro-organisms at the same time. If you are confident that your own garden soil is free of soil-borne pests and diseases then sterilisation may be a waste of time. However, if you are making your own compost mix using ingredients from your own garden you may wish to consider sterilisation options, especially if you are making seed or cutting compost, young plants being more vulnerable than more mature plants.

To sterilise small amounts of soil or homemade compost in a microwave oven, fill a thick plastic bag with around 1kg (2½lb) of moist soil or compost, leave the top open and place in the centre of the oven. Heat for around 2–3 minutes in a thick plastic bag. Ideally the soil should be heated to temperatures of around 82–93°C (180–200°F). For hygiene and safety reasons, avoid using your domestic kitchen microwave for sterilising composts, and don't place metal bowls, dishes or utensils in them.

For larger amounts of compost or soil, using the power of the sun is the best option. Spread your mix 10cm (4in) deep on a sheet of plastic in a place that receives full sun, moisten with plenty of water and cover with a another sheet of clear plastic, weighted down. In hot, sunny weather the soil should 'bake' adequately in about four weeks, but the process will take longer in cloudier, cooler conditions. Fork the mix over once a week to ensure the sun gets to all parts.

TYPES OF
COMPOSTING
SYSTEMS

CLOSED OR OPEN SYSTEMS?

Essentially, there are two main methods of composting, closed or open systems, but there are variations of each.

The closed system is where the amount of air and moisture is controlled by you. Closed systems usually take up little space and are ideal for small gardens, particularly patios and courtyards, as there shouldn't be any material leaching out from the bottom of the bin, looking unsightly. They usually warm up faster and retain the heat better than open systems, and have a lid to keep out rain. There are some very trendy-looking, 'designer' closed compost bin systems that can actually become an attractive feature in the garden.

The open system of composting is where the material is fairly open to the elements, so weather conditions such as rain, sunshine and wind can all speed up the decomposition process. Examples of such a method could be as simple as a pile of compostable material in the corner of the garden, lasagne planting (see page 43), or composting using pallets. Some gardeners put a tarpaulin over their heaps to prevent too much of the material leaching or washing away into the ground. The advantage of the open system is that heaps can be made as big as you like, and are very cheap to create. The disadvantage is that they take up a fair amount of space, and can look unsightly and a bit messy if they aren't tucked away in a sheltered corner of the garden.

CLOSED SYSTEMS

Daleks

The 'dalek' bin is probably the most commonly used method of composting in small-to-medium gardens. Daleks are made of plastic and are cylindrical in shape, tapering inwards towards the lid at the top. There is a sliding door towards the bottom, which can be opened to remove the material once it has rotted down. It may be necessary to make bins rodent-proof by attaching a thin wire mesh across the base to prevent rats and mice burrowing underneath and up into the compost. Daleks are cheap and easily available. Some local authorities even provide them for free to encourage people to compost their garden and kitchen waste, reducing down the amount of material having to be collected by refuse collectors.

Place chicken wire or mesh underneath closed compost bins to keep out rats and mice.

A compost bin that gets hot will decompose material far quicker than a cold, wet compost heap.

Hot compost systems

Scientists and compost gurus will tell you that the warmer the compost heap is, the quicker it will break down waste. A compost heap hot enough to destroy weed seedlings, diseases and pests, and to process waste speedily without overheating and killing off the composting micro-organisms, requires considerable effort to achieve in an ordinary garden. Layering, endless turning, combining ingredients in specific ways and a fair amount of space are needed, so this tends to be the province of the seriously committed.

However, scientific and practical research has recently been applied to products that are much better suited to modern living, using some basic principles on a smaller scale for people with limited space and time. It is now increasingly possible to buy specially designed compost containers that allow small amounts of waste to be processed on a regular basis, producing usable compost from waste in a short space of time. Search online for 'hot compost systems' to find a variety of brands.

They all share similar features. Made of materials that are insulating, such as polypropylene, and being compact and attractive, they can be placed close to the back door or on a balcony, and if well managed are efficient managers of waste. The regulated heat can destroy bacteria and pests so it is possible, if you really want to, to compost pet waste, cooked meat and dairy products, even human waste. In most cases, however, kitchen waste and paper or cardboard are the usual components. Look for hot containers that have integral design features, such as a thermometer, drainage and aeration systems, to help you manage your compost process more easily. They are perfect for urban gardens.

Wheelie bin compost bin

Wheelie bins are ideal containers for transforming into compost bins. Their compact size and upright shape means that even people with the smallest of gardens can fit one in somewhere, ideally close to the kitchen door. To turn an ordinary wheelie bin into a compost bin, drill holes about 5cm (2in) apart in the sides and underneath to allow the air to circulate through the bin.

This will speed up the decomposition process. It doesn't matter how large the air holes are, but if they're bigger than 1cm (½in) wide, it may be worth lining the inside of the bin to prevent rodent problems. There is very little else to it, really. Fill the bin with kitchen and garden waste. Avoid adding meats and dairy products as the compost heap probably won't get hot enough for them to decompose fully. Every few days, when you're walking past, give the bin a shake or rock it forwards and back on its wheels to circulate air and turn the material over. When you're ready to use the compost, simply lie the wheelie bin on its side, open the lid and dig out all that lovely, decomposed material. The compost is ready when it is a dark brown, almost black colour, and the texture is slightly friable to the touch. It will usually take more than a year to reach this stage, but it will depend on what material has been placed in the bin, and outside temperatures.

Rotating compost containers

Rotating compost containers are great labour-saving devices. Instead of having to turn the compost with a spade, a handle is turned which rotates the compost heap for you. There are some extremely useful models available to buy, and some of them look great in the garden too. One popular model has two drums side by side, so that one can be used for filling with fresh compost, while the one next to it can be regularly turned until it decomposes.

If you've got some basic practical skills you can make your own rotating compost container by securely impaling a plastic barrel onto a horizontal wooden post. Alternatively, a simple plastic dustbin can be used to make a rotating compost bin. As with the wheelie bin mentioned previously, drill holes through the sides and underneath of the bin, and line with wire gauge if the holes are large enough for rodents to get through. Start filling with compostable material. The advantage of a round plastic dustbin is that it can be easily laid on its side and rolled around to aerate the compost. This is much easier than having to turn the compost with a spade. Use a bungee for securing the lid to prevent the material spilling out.

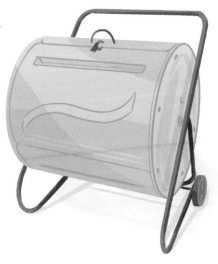

A rotating compost bin saves you having to 'turn' the compost with a fork to aerate it and speed up decomposition.

Keyhole gardening is based on a raised bed with a central compost heap that gradually leaches out nutrients into the soil to feed the plants.

OPEN SYSTEMS

Keyhole gardening

This is a simple and innovative way to make a compost heap, while at the same time creating an attractive raised flower or vegetable bed.

The concept was developed in Africa but has now become a globally recognised sustainable composting model. It began as a system for people to create their own food crops sustainably, using little or no money and just the resources they had in their surrounding landscapes.

The idea is to create a circular raised bed built out of rocks or local stone, with a gap or cleft cut out of the circle, and a path leading to a compost heap in the centre of the bed. This cleft creates an easy route for the gardener to access the central compost heap in the centre of the raised bed. The compost heap can be made from natural, permeable material such as rushes, straw or grass. The theory is that kitchen and garden waste are placed onto the compost heap, and this leaches out and into the raised bed. The nutrients and material from the compost heap help feed the plants and provide additional moisture. It helps the leaching process if the centre of the bed is slightly higher than the outer bed area, and gradually slopes towards the edges, as gravity can then work towards sending the composted material to the furthest areas. This system encourages strong, healthy crops, which can then be cut back after they've finished cropping and placed back into the central compost heap to biodegrade and provide compost for the next season of crops. In this way, it is a completely sustainable system of gardening. Building a series of small, raised keyhole gardens in an outdoor space enables gardeners to practise crop rotation, moving each type of crop to a different bed each year, helping to prevent a build-up of pests and disease in the soil.

Hugelkultur

Nearly always, nature knows best, and hugelkultur is another method of gardening that harnesses the slow natural decomposition of woody plant material to its advantage. It originated in northern Europe, and the literal translation of the name means 'hill or mound culture'. It involves covering logs, branches and other carbon material such as straw and cardboard with mounds of soil. The very slow decomposition of the underlying wood and organic matter feeds the roots of the plants growing on top of the mound. Based on a type of no-dig method, hugelkultur reduces the need for watering or irrigation systems as the logs and branches act like a sponge, holding onto rainwater and releasing it during dry spells. Another benefit is that the decomposing material below eliminates the need for fertilisers, while the benefit of mounded and sloping raised beds increases the surface area for growing. It is estimated that the constant supply of nutrients as the material breaks down could last for 20 years.

Straw bales

For shorter-term gardening or smaller spaces, straw bales can be used in a similar way to the hugelkultur system described above, harnessing the decomposition of carbon-rich straw, which, as it breaks down, provides nutrients to the plants that are planted in the bale. Use a garden knife to cut out planting holes in the bale, each one being around twice the size of the rootball. Fill the bottom of the hole with garden compost, place the plant in the hole and firm it in with compost pushed down the sides. Regularly water the bale during dry periods with water collected from a water butt, and eventually the plants will send out roots into the straw bale itself. As in hugelkultur, the decomposing straw holds onto moisture and releases it when the plant is in need. A quick online search will provide a list of suppliers who can deliver straw bales.

No-dig gardening

No dig horticulture is an increasingly popular method that reflects our growing understanding of the complex life in the soil, not, as has been sometimes suggested, simply an excuse offered by lazy gardeners to avoid hard work. At first, this system may appear to go against many gardeners' and farmers' initial instincts, which are to dig, turn over the soil, rotovate or plough before planting.

One of the main reasons gardeners dig their soil is to remove weeds. The basic premise of no-dig gardening is that by not digging over your soil, you disrupt the life present in it less and expose fewer dormant weed seeds to the conditions they need to germinate. Instead of digging, the no-dig system relies on regularly adding layers of compostable material to the surface of the soil, which should eventually result in a rich, friable, crumbly soil.

In soil that has been previously cultivated you would need to apply at least 15cm (6in) of compost over the top. Over time, organisms such as worms will move in and consume this material, adding to the richness of the soil beneath, so there is no need to dig it in.

If your compost is already well decomposed you can directly plant or sow immediately – simply rake the surface to a fine tilth as usual. Any weeds should be easy to deal with as they pull out of the soft surface and crumbly soil beneath with little resistance. In general, annual weed germination will be reduced considerably, while perennial weeds may take longer to tackle, although their roots become easier to pull out as time goes on. If your compost is less well decomposed it is better to leave it for a month or two before planting, since the decomposition process can temporarily deplete the soil of essential nutrients. The layer of mulch then simply needs topping up annually, in autumn or spring.

A thick layer of compost can also be used to clear an area of weeds, either spread so thickly (at least 15cm [6in] deep) that the weeds underneath cannot find light, or used in conjunction with another sort of light-excluding covering, such as cardboard, weed-control fabric or an organic mulch like straw and grass clippings.

The aim is simple – to exclude light and create a soft layer that perennial weed roots can more easily be removed from. It may take up to a year to weaken the most robust and deep-rooted perennials, such as dock, bramble and bindweed, but with patience you can clear a space relatively easily and be left with wonderful fertile soil.

Lasagne planting

Another no-dig method of using decomposing material to aid plant growth is called lasagne planting. Lasagne beds have very little to do with the classic Italian dish except for the fact that the sheets of cardboard used in this method resemble its layers. Flattened cardboard is placed over a bed, and organic material is then placed on top, followed by another layer of cardboard, then another layer of compostable material, and so on, to build up a raised bed. Plants are planted into the cardboard, which acts as a mulch to suppress weeds and helps to retain moisture by acting like a sponge. Each year, the decomposing material is left on the beds, and more layers of cardboard and organic material are added, building up the beds into a nutrient-rich flower bed. Once the beds are established they are superb at retaining moisture, but in the early days, they may need watering to help the cardboard decompose and, of course, to keep the plants happy.

Raised beds

One of the most popular uses for homemade compost is for filling up raised beds. It is possible to import lots of topsoil from a garden centre, but filling beds with pure, homemade compost is a much cheaper and easier option, and enables you to grow your plants directly into a highly nutritious and healthy growing medium. Each year the beds will need topping up with more compost, which is easy if you are making your own. Most raised beds are made from timber, but they can also be made from bricks, stone and even rubber tyres.

Benefits of using raised beds

- The height of a raised bed saves back-breaking work as less stretching is required and weeding, planting and sowing takes place at a much more comfortable height.
- If you have poor soil (or even no soil), then raised beds can be filled with compost to improve growing conditions.
- Drainage is far better in a raised bed than in beds on the ground.
- Raised beds warm up faster in the springtime than the rest of the beds in the garden.

Direct planting into the compost

Probably the simplest method of growing plants using homemade compost is just to plant them on top of the compost heap. This is particularly effective with pumpkin and squash plants, which are hungry feeders and thrive in the warm, fertile conditions of a compost heap. The one disadvantage, of course, is that the remainder of the compost heap can't be used on the garden while pumpkins are growing in it. However, once the pumpkin has finished fruiting, the compost underneath can still be spread on the beds as a mulch.

Traditionally, too, vegetable gardeners sometimes dig out a trench in winter and throw their kitchen waste directly into it, along with thin layers of soil, before planting out runner beans in early summer, by which time the trench will be a rich source of nutrients for these hungry plants.

MAKING A WIRE-BASED COMPOST BIN

Composting shouldn't be expensive. Some bespoke bins can set you back a few hundred pounds, but a compost heap can cost you next to nothing if you're happy to make it yourself and are not too fussed about how it looks. There are many materials that can be recycled and made into a bin. Search around warehouses or factories, as there are often wooden crates sitting outside that are going spare (always ask before you take anything though). Wooden crates can simply be wrapped in wire gauge around the sides to hold in any garden or kitchen waste, and instantly you have a compost bin.

If you can't get your hands on an old crate, then an even simpler method is to bang four corner posts into the ground to form a 1m (approximately 3¼ft) square. Wrap wire gauge around the back and two sides of the posts leaving the front free from wire for ease of access. Attach the wire gauge using a hammer and staples, and you have a very cheap yet functional compost heap, ready to be filled with garden waste, which probably only took 15 minutes to make.

Old foldable wire pet cages used to take animals to the vets can be recycled and make excellent small composting containers for small gardens. Their size means they can be slotted into the tiniest of spaces, while the wire material that makes up the sides and roof are perfect for holding the material in place. The gaps between the wire enable air to circulate, which speeds up the process of decomposition. The base of the compost heap is solid, ensuring not too much of the compost leaches away when it rains. In addition there is a convenient 'door' to get the compost in and out. Once it has been emptied, it can be folded away for easy storage until it is needed again.

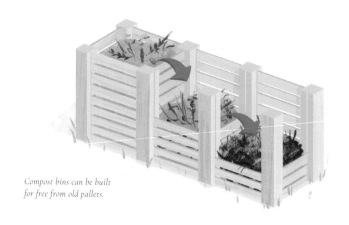

Compost bins can be built for free from old pallets.

MAKING A PALLET COMPOST FACILITY

Making a composting facility from old pallets is one of the cheapest methods of recycling your garden and kitchen waste. It is easy to do and is practically free if you can get your hands on some old pallets. You can often find stacks of them around the back of warehouses or factories, but do ask first, as some are reused or returned to where they originally came from for a refund.

The image above shows three separate bays for composting. Bay One, on the left, is the one in which you would first place your kitchen waste. Once it is full, the material in it is 'turned' into Bay Two, the middle one, freeing up Bay One for new garden waste.

When Bay One becomes full for the second time, the contents of Bay Two are turned into Bay Three, on the right, where it is left until it is ready to use. Bay One would be emptied into Bay Two, leaving Bay One empty to be filled up with new compost. Once the rotted compost in Bay Three is used in the garden, then the cycle starts again, with Bay Two being emptied into Bay Three and Bay One emptied into Bay Two. Bay One would once again be free to receive fresh garden and kitchen waste.

One of the advantages of pallet composting facilities is that they provide easy access due to the large width of the bays, making it handy to transfer wheelbarrows full of garden waste in and out of them. If you are short of space, you can just make one or two bays for composting, but the ideal number is three; one for using on the garden, one for resting and one for filling up with current garden waste. The compost bays should be next to each other as it makes it easier to turn the compost from one into another due to their proximity, and also uses up fewer pallets since they share adjoining walls.

To make three bays you will need:
- Seven pallets of the same size for the back and sides of the bays
- Three half-size pallets for the front
- A saw to cut the front pallets in half
- Bailer twine or garden wire and wire cutters.

Ideally the compost should be sited on soil or an old lawn as the decomposing material will draw worms and microbes up into the compost. However, it can be placed on a patio or concrete if there is no other option. Avoid placing it on decking, however.

Most pallets are 1.2m (4ft) in length, so to accommodate a three-bay pallet facility you will need enough space for the length of three pallets and the depth of one.

First clear the ground of any perennial weeds, such as ground elder, nettle or bindweed, as these will grow up into your compost and become very difficult to eradicate.

If space allows, have two or three compost bays, so one bay can decompose while you fill another with fresh material.

Building your bays

Start by building the first bay. Place three pallets on their lengthways edge to form an open-sided rectangle with two sides and the back. If you want to make a really sturdy structure you can bang posts in at the corners to prop the pallets upright and then screw the pallets to them. However, most pallets will be sturdy enough without them. Pallets can be attached together with small, stainless steel brackets on the inside of the corners. An even cheaper version is to simply lash the corners of the pallets together with wire or bailer twine. This is particularly suitable if you only envisage the compost bays being in place for a couple of years.

Next, build the adjoining two bays, by simply attaching two more 'backs' and two more pallets between the bays, again using either brackets or twine to hold them together.

'Front doors'

A 'front' on the compost bays can be useful to prevent all the compost spilling outwards. However, it needs to be easily removable to provide ready access. To achieve this, cut three pallets in half to make the three 'fronts'. Full-size pallets can be used, but these are heavier to move every time you want to access the compost heap. To keep the half-pallets upright against the compost bays, measure the thickness of the pallet, which is usually about 20cm (8in), although pallets will vary. Then bang in four stout, upright stakes at the front end of each wall of the bays, leaving a 20cm (8in) gap. You can then slot the half-pallets between the stakes and the three compost bays to form the removable 'fronts'. Alternatively, you can fit hinges so that the doors swing open, as shown below.

The 'doors' on these bays have been made by creating frames with wire mesh stretched over them and then hung on hinges.

Brick compost bins

For a more permanent structure that will last longer than timber, bricks make an excellent choice. They can be built to a similar size and shape as the three-bay wooden pallet compost facility discussed on the previous pages, but will be far more durable. The bricks would need to be mortared together using cement, and shallow footings would be required to prevent it from sinking.

An alternative structure that doesn't require footings or cementing is a temporary circular brick structure. This was a popular method in Victorian times, and is a quick and easy project to try. It's ideal if you have surplus bricks in your garden or can salvage some out of a skip. The rustic appearance of this compost structure makes a great feature in a garden too. The gaps left between the bricks allows air to circulate, meaning it isn't necessary to turn the compost.

To make a circular, rustic compost structure:

1. Level out the ground where you intend to build your structure.
2. Using a stick, mark out a circle about 1.5m (5ft) in diameter in the soil.
3. Lay bricks on the ground in the shape of the circle, leaving a gap between each one.
4. Start the next tier of bricks, staggering them so that they fit over the gaps below, and leaving a gap from each other.
5. Repeat these steps until your structure is about 1m (3¼ft) high.

Compost bins made from bricks can be used to make a sturdier and more permanent feature in the garden.

You can then fill your brick structure with composted material. Cover with cardboard or a tarpaulin and leave for a year. When you are ready to use the compost, simply remove the bricks to access it.

If you wish to create a more permanent structure, you can mortar the bricks together, but leave a gap at the base wide enough for you to shovel out the compost once it has decomposed. While you are cementing the bricks together, it is possible to lean them inwards slightly on each row to form an attractive beehive-shaped composter.

Bespoke or self-build timber compost kits

Build-it-yourself compost kits are a good compromise for those gardeners who want an open compost system but would like something smarter-looking than just recycled pallets. There are lots of systems available, but almost all of them are made from timber. Many comprise modular elements that can be added on as the compost system expands. Many of them are very easy to build, requiring minimal DIY skills. Before purchasing, check that the timber is from a sustainable source, and if it has been treated, that an environmentally friendly product has been used.

Weave your own compost container

If you have a willow, hazel or dogwood growing in the garden, it is possible to make a very simple yet effective compost container from their woven stems. Use secateurs to remove the one-year-old stems that are over 1m (3¼ft) long from the shrub to make the sides of the compost container. Do this when the plant is dormant (once the leaves have fallen, between autumn and early spring). If you don't have any of these stems in your garden, they can be purchased online.

To make a woven compost container, mark out a 1.2m (4ft) diameter circle in the soil where it is going to be built. Bang hazel stakes into the ground at intervals of 20cm (8in) around the edge of the circle so they are 1m (3¼ft) high above ground. Then use supple, one-year-old stems from willow, hazel or dogwood and, starting at the bottom, weave the 'rods' or 'withies' between the upright stakes until the top is reached. The withies can be made more flexible by soaking them overnight in water, such as in the bath or a pond. Brightly coloured cornus stems look extremely striking, but the colour fades after a year. The structure will usually last for two or three years before it will all need replacing.

Making a turf stack

Very often in gardens, turf is lifted to create flower beds, paths or patios, and this leaves the problem of having to dispose of the turves. Thankfully, old turves can make superb compost if made into a stack and left for a couple of years to rot down.

To make a turf stack:

1. Using a tuft lifter or spade, remove the turf from the area of lawn you wish to clear, to a depth of about 3cm (1¼in).
2. Using a spade, cut the removed turf into sections of about 30 × 30cm (12 × 12in).
3. Clear a space of about 1m (3¼ft) square in a sunny spot of the garden, and stack the turves in it by laying them on top of one another, with the grass side facing downwards.
4. Water the stack and then cover with a tarpaulin. Leave for about two years, and then use as either a potting compost or as mulch on your beds.

Compost toilets are useful when there are no drains or running water available, such as in some community gardens or allotments.

COMPOST TOILETS

The composting process has a rather practical, if less pleasant, application that is currently gaining in popularity. Compost loos have been in use for hundreds of years in countries such as China, but are a more recent and growing addition to the British landscape. Also called biological or waterless toilets, they are an efficient method of recycling human waste into compost material that goes back into the soil, using the same micro-organisms and process that you find in your garden compost heap. As they do not use water and produce no by-product other than compost, they are useful when sewerage and water systems are not available, and are especially popular with those who aim to be self-sufficient.

The internet is full of DIY designs for allotmenteers and smallholders but it is also possible to buy well-designed commercial compost toilet systems that minimise the risk to human health and environment. Whichever system is used, an important objective is to destroy any pathogens, either by leaving for a long time or heating to a high enough temperature.

Making your own basic compost toilet

1. Create a structure for privacy, such as fencing or trellis, or use an existing shed.
2. Within or behind the structure, secure a toilet seat for comfort over a plastic dustbin.
3. Line the bottom of the dustbin with 5cm (2in) of fine sawdust. Sawdust or shavings can be purchased from farm supply shops, poultry-rearing suppliers or pet shops (it is used for rabbit or guinea pig bedding). You could also ask a local carpenter if they have surplus sawdust.
4. After using the toilet facilities sprinkle sawdust over the top of it. As a rule of thumb – one scoop for pees, two scoops for poops (one scoop is equivalent to a small shovelful).
5. Biodegradable toilet paper can also be added to the compost toilet.
6. When the bin is full, it can be emptied into a hole or pit.
7. When the pit is full, cover with soil, and leave the pit to decompose for at least a year. Activated charcoal can also be added into the pit to help neutralise the decomposing material. Always purchase from sustainable and reputable suppliers.
8. After a year or two, it can be used on flower beds, although it is best to avoid using on vegetable and fruit beds.

HOW TO
MAKE
COMPOST

THE SCIENCE
BEHIND THE ART OF
COMPOSTING

The process of composting is generally a simple one, and the reality is that nature does most of the work. As many of us will have discovered when looking at food in the fridge that has gone past its best-before or use-by date, organic waste, if left to its own devices, will eventually decompose or rot on its own without anyone needing to intervene at all. This is due to micro-organisms all around us completing their life cycle.

As organic bodies – whether plant or animal – die, their components are gradually and inevitably broken down to create new life. Composting is really only a way of speeding up and controlling the process of decomposition by providing good conditions for waste-eating organisms to thrive. As long as you provide food, warmth, moisture and oxygen you will inevitably achieve your end goal of usable compost sooner or later.

Having said that, a little more understanding of the composting process and the behaviour and needs of the micro-organisms that you are harnessing may help you to improve your composting performance.

Scientific researchers have spent plenty of time working out what actually goes on in the composting process and have identified three separate stages in which different types of micro-organisms do their thing.

Composting: stage 1

The first stage typically lasts only a few days. Micro-organisms, which thrive in temperatures of between 20 and 45°C (68–113°F), quickly start to break down organic compounds, producing a variety of acids, carbon dioxide and heat. These are known as mesophilic micro-organisms and they work best when temperatures are around 30°C 86°F). However, as heat is a by-product of their digesting activity, temperatures will quickly start to rise in the compost heap to levels that encourage different kinds of micro-organisms to take over.

Composting: stage 2

Mesophilic micro-organisms are replaced by heat-loving micro-organisms, known as thermophilic microbes, during the second stage, which can last from a few days to several months. These micro-organisms specialise in breaking down compounds into ever finer pieces and can digest proteins, fats and complex carbohydrates.

During this period temperatures can continue to rise and may get to levels that even the heat-loving microbes cannot cope with, effectively killing them off.

Aeration and turning will help to keep the temperature below 65°C (149°F), and many committed composters make sure that they turn their compost regularly at this early stage to extend the activity period of these organisms, giving them a fresh injection of food and oxygen and cooling the heap down.

Composting: stage 3

The third and final stage, which typically lasts for several months to a year, is a slower and cooler process. When the heat-loving micro-organisms have used up all the available resources, temperatures drop again, allowing other kinds of micro-organisms to work once more, breaking down any remaining organic matter into smaller and smaller pieces. This is also the time when bigger organisms may take up residence in your compost heap.

Generally, it is taken for granted that the higher temperatures produced by all this microbe activity are necessary to kill any pathogens, seeds and perennial plants that may end up in your compost. Scientists have discovered that a temperature of 50°C (122°F) for 24 hours is enough to kill any pathogens present, while slightly lower temperatures will be just as effective but take longer. Some even go so far as to point out that given enough time all pathogens will eventually die, regardless of the temperature.

If, for whatever reason, your compost doesn't seem to be heating up, then don't despair. It is not only heat that kills anything nasty but a combination of other factors that also help. The compost micro-organisms themselves are a tough bunch and can often outcompete a pathogen, consuming or fighting it, even producing natural antibiotics to deal with them, so it is very unlikely that your compost will contain anything too harmful when you use it on a vegetable bed, for example. A colder composting process will simply take a little longer. Unless you are determined to compost pet or human waste and meat-based food, your compost should be perfectly safe to use around the garden, however it has been processed.

MICROBIAL AEROBICS

Micro-organisms such as bacteria and fungi account for nearly all the decomposition that takes place in a compost heap. They are separated into two main types, known as aerobes and anaerobes.

Aerobes

Composting aerobes are micro-organisms that, like us, require oxygen to survive. They are the most important and most efficient consumers of organic waste, converting it into the simple building blocks of life, like nitrogen and phosphorus, and they are everywhere in huge numbers. One gram of healthy soil or compost will contain millions of these microscopic creatures and they can eat pretty much everything. They break up complex organic material by oxidising it, needing the carbon molecules to create energy, and nitrogen to build the proteins that they require to grow and reproduce. It is the oxidation process that creates heat as a by-product.

When they have consumed and used what they need to survive, they excrete the leftovers as plant nutrients, the simple chemicals such as nitrogen, phosphorus and potassium that will feed your plants.

While these bacteria can eat a wide variety of organic compounds, they are unable to cope with unfavourable conditions, due to their minuscule size and simplicity. Oxygen levels below 5 per cent and less than ideal levels of moisture, temperature and acidity may cause them to die off, slowing decomposition by as much as 90 per cent.

Anaerobes

When oxygen levels are low, another major type of micro-organism gets its chance to shine. Anaerobic micro-organisms are bacteria that don't require oxygen. They are less efficient processors of waste, bind nitrogen so that it becomes unusable, and often produce chemical substances that can be toxic to plants. They also produce some awful smells including ammonia, hydrogen sulphide, which smells like rotten eggs, and cadaverine and putrescine, odours that are more than aptly named.

High numbers of anaerobic microbes are usually the cause of smelly and slimy compost heaps, hence the need to oxygenate and turn compost to maximise aerobic rather than anaerobic activity.

The importance of humus in soil

Traditionally, soil has been seen as something rather lifeless, a layer of ground-up rock and debris in which plant roots access water and basic nutrients. In truth, the thin layers of soil that cover the planet are absolutely full of life, and are far more complex than we could ever imagine.

The three main components of soil are all necessary for successful growing. Firstly, ground-up rock provides essential minerals, structure and drainage. Secondly, organic matter (known as humus) holds water, provides nutrients, keeps the soil open and provides a home for the third component, billions of soil-dwelling organisms that feed, excrete and convert complex chemical ingredients into the simple building blocks of life.

Whatever type of soil you have in your garden, whether sandy and rocky, chalk, clay or silt, the addition of humus-rich homemade compost, in whatever form, will help improve performance.

COMPOSTING ISSUES

Creepy-crawlies in your bin

The larger creatures that you might find when you open the lid of your bin or turn your heap, such as worms, millipedes, slugs and snails and beetles, help the process along in a different way, by consuming and excreting materials into smaller pieces, a more physical action. They are a useful addition to your compost heap, so in most cases can be left in situ. However, keep an eye out when you are spreading your compost on your beds and pick out and dispose of any slugs and snails that have hitched a ride. Leave the rest for the birds to feast on. Robins are usually quick to spot a compost spreader at work and make the most of the opportunity. Chickens, too, if you have them, thoroughly enjoy scratching through a pile of compost for food, and many people empty their compost bin onto a groundsheet first to facilitate this.

In larger, open heaps you may possibly find one or two other squatters. Hedgehogs and slow-worms are quite fond of bedding down in compost heaps, so do check first before moving or turning it.

When to compost?

Composting can be done all year round, as and when you have garden or kitchen waste available. Generally, more green material from the garden is produced from mid-summer to late autumn and woody stems and prunings in winter.

Size matters

Open compost bins should be at least 1m × 1m × 1m (approximately 3¼ft × 3¼ft × 3¼ft). Any smaller and there won't be enough room to turn the heap effectively and it won't be large enough to warm up.

You can influence how efficiently your compost heap decomposes in the following ways:

- Creating a well-balanced mix of carbon- and nitrogen-based material.
- Ensuring there is adequate airflow, warmth and moisture within the heap.
- Managing the heap by regularly turning it.
- Chopping up or shredding material. A few bulkier items, though, such as egg boxes and scrunched-up newspaper, will increase airflow.
- Adding accelerators to it (optional). See page 71 for information on accelerators.
- Kitchen waste – a caddy kept in the kitchen for vegetable or fruit peelings is useful for managing your waste. Biodegradable bags can be used to line the caddy, and then added to rot in the compost heap. (Note: Keep meat, fish and dairy products in a separate food caddy and don't add to the garden compost unless you have a hot bin that has reached at least 50°C (122°F) and is rodent-proof.)

What to add to your compost heap

As a rule of thumb, a good compost heap should consist of a mix of green (nitrogen-rich) and brown (carbon-based) material. A mix of nitrogen-rich and carbon-based material provides the best environment for the bacteria and micro-organisms that are necessary for decomposition to take place. Exact ratios are difficult to give as it depends on the richness and type of materials used, but about two-thirds green material and one-third brown material is a good target to aim for. Some plant and kitchen waste may contain varying amounts of both green and brown material, so adjustments will have to be made where necessary, especially if the compost heap isn't efficiently breaking down. Ideally, brown and green are added in layers, but this isn't always practical in terms of when compostable material is available unless you are willing to store it to one side separately until you are ready to make up your heap.

- **Green material** includes grass clippings, kitchen waste (such as vegetable peelings, fruit, used coffee granules and teabags), herbaceous material and seaweed.
- **Brown material** includes wood chippings, sawdust, straw, hay, newspaper, shredded paper, shredded cardboard, old grass stems and shredded twigs.

Kitchen waste is a good source of green material.

Getting your materials to your compost bin

Biodegradable bags make transporting your compost from the kitchen caddy inside your house to the compost bin outside much easier than having to shake out non-disposable bags of kitchen waste into the compost. Instead, simply place biodegradable bags directly on to the top of the compost heap and let them decompose there. Brown paper bags or even rolled-up newspaper can also be used to collect together kitchen waste in the house if the food isn't too moist, or has been left indoors too long.

Various compostable materials have different decomposition speeds:

- **Fast** Nettles, comfrey, grass, blood and bone meal, fruit and vegetable peelings
- **Medium** Straw, coffee grounds, teabags, nuts, cardboard
- **Slow** Eggshells, wood chippings, twigs, shredded leaves

Adding fresh perennial weeds to the compost heap should be avoided, as the roots will love growing into the compost and infiltrating the entire compost heap. Once this has happened it is very difficult to eradicate them. Some of the more common perennial plants to avoid include:

- bindweed
- ground elder
- perennial stinging nettle
- Japanese knotweed
- bamboo
- dandelion
- couch grass
- oxalis
- celandine
- enchanter's nightshade
- creeping buttercup
- creeping thistle
- horsetail (mare's tail)
- dock leaves

If you would rather recycle your perennial weeds in a compost heap instead of taking them to the recycling centre, there are four methods available.

- **Burning** Perennial weeds can be burnt in a small incinerator and the ashes added to the compost.
- **Bagging them up** Place perennial roots into dustbin bags, tie up the ends to exclude light and leave them to die in a corner for about six months before adding them to the compost heap.
- **Drying out the roots** This method relies on warm weather so is most effective in the summer. Perennial roots should be left outside in the sunshine, either on the lid of the composter or on a hard surface such as the patio. Using a hammer to break up the roots will speed up the process. Leave the roots to desiccate in the sun for a few weeks until they turn brittle. They can then be added to the compost.
- **Drowning** Place the plants in a bucket and soak the roots for up to a year to turn them into a sludge, then add the contents to the compost. See page 83 for more details.

Accelerators and activators

Your average open compost system will take about a year to produce good compost. However, if you can't wait that long, there are products that will speed up the process. Some contain high levels of nitrogen (compost accelerators), others carbon (compost activators), and so can be used to help balance shortages in either green or brown material. For application follow the manufacturer's guidelines.

DO ADD

- **Eggshells** Smash the shells up into small pieces and scatter them into the compost. They're a good source of calcium for plants. Avoid eggshells if your bin isn't rodent-proof, unless you are willing to wash them thoroughly.

- **Fruit** If possible, chop up large whole fruits such as apples and pears into smaller pieces. Smaller fruits, such as grapes, currants and gooseberries, are fine if added whole. Avoid too many citrus fruits like oranges and lemons, which can make the compost acidic.
- **Wood chippings and shredded branches** This bulky material will allow air to circulate within the heap, as well as providing a source of carbon, but it can be slow to break down.
- **Autumn leaves** Leaves can be slow to rot, but the process will be much faster if you shred them first.
- **Shredded newspaper** A great source of carbon and perfect for adding to compost if it is too 'green' and slimy. Scrunch up some newspaper to create pockets of air to speed up decomposition.
- **Vegetable peelings and salad leaves** A great source of nitrogen and will rot quickly and add nutrients for future plants that will be grown in the compost. Avoid adding strongly flavoured onions and chillies in large quantities.

- **Garden clippings** If possible, chop garden clippings up as small as possible to speed up decomposition. A good source of green, nitrogen-rich material.
- **Brown cardboard** A good source of carbon to balance against nitrogen-rich materials, such as grass clippings and herbaceous garden material.
- **Fireplace ash from wood** A good source of potassium, although it doesn't retain these benefits for long. Ash also contains other trace nutrients. It can be quite alkaline, so is useful if your compost has become too acidic, but don't add too much as it will increase the pH level excessively. Avoid adding ashes from pre-made barbecue grills, however, as they can have chemical residues. Also to be avoided is ash from timber that has been treated.
- **Rotted chicken, cow and horse manure** This bulky material will enhance your garden compost.
- **Bedding waste from pets such as rabbits and hamsters** Carbon-rich bedding mixed with animal waste is a potent accelerator.

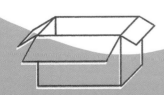

DON'T ADD

- **Bones and meat** Cooked bones can be added to hot compost systems, if temperatures will get hot enough for them to decompose. Break them up first with a hammer into small pieces, and only add if your compost bin is rodent-proof. Avoid adding them to standard domestic compost heaps, though, as the cooler temperature means they will take a long time to break down and will start to smell, which will attract rodents and foxes, as well as making it unpleasant for yourself and your neighbours.
- **Silver foil and wrapping paper** Avoid adding these as they contain chemicals and additives.
- **Milk and dairy products** These are very rich in calcium, but should be avoided unless you are using a hot compost system, due to their smell and extreme alkalinity. They will also attract rodents.
- **Cat litter and dog poo** Avoid putting pet faeces into the compost as they contain unhealthy bacterias and micro-organisms. This is particularly important if the compost is then going to be used on soil to grow edible crops.
- **Glossy magazines** The paper used in magazines often contains plastic and other synthetic materials to make it glossy. The bright ink used can also be toxic.

- **Fruit label stickers** Remove labels from fruit before adding them to the compost as they don't decompose easily.
- **Oils** Best avoided as they won't decompose properly and will make your compost greasy. Coating your compost with oils (even cooking or vegetable oils) will prevent the other compost materials from decomposing and will harm worms and other micro-organisms needed for the compost to work.
- **Coal ash** Coal is treated, and the ash should therefore be avoided.
- **Material that has been treated with chemicals** such as weed killer, fungicide and insecticide.
- **Any non-organic material.**

Teabags

Teabags are sometimes made of thin layers of a type of plastic, in which case they shouldn't be composted. Tea leaves and biodegradable bags are fine.

Use a fork to 'turn' the compost every few weeks to aerate the material and speed up decomposition.

Turning compost

The more air the compost heap receives, the faster the material will break down. Compost heaps should always have air holes in their sides to encourage airflow, but the best way to aerate a heap is to turn it. This involves digging out the material and restacking it. Ideally you should try to re-form your heap with the outside, least composted colder sections swapping position with the better-composted, warmer middle. If you only have one bay, then you'll have to double-handle it, by turning it out and then turning it back in. If you have more than one heap then you can simply transfer directly from one to the other.

It isn't absolutely necessary to turn a compost heap, particularly if you have a good mix of brown and green material, but it can certainly speed things along. Turn the heap as often as you can throughout the year. Professional gardeners will often turn their heap once a month.

Troubleshooting

A properly made compost heap should warm up as material decomposes. Compost heaps shouldn't be smelly or slimy. If that is the case then there is probably too much green (nitrogen-rich) material in there. This is often the case when large amounts of fresh grass clippings are added all at once, creating a smelly pancake that smothers everything else and deprives the compost heap of air. A quick fix solution is to add wood chippings, newspaper or cardboard (brown material) and dig it in, which will also aerate the soil and speed up the decomposition.

If the compost heap is too dry and isn't breaking down, there is probably too much brown or carbon-rich material in it. Try adding more nitrogen and a splash of rainwater.

A question of balance

Making good compost involves treading a thin line between too dry or too wet. Place a bin in full sun if you want your material to break down faster, as a hot compost will decompose quickly in the heat. But you'll need to remember to water it occasionally. Don't let the heap dry out completely as the micro-organisms need moisture to thrive. As a guide, the compost material should be like a damp sponge to the touch.

How do you know when the compost is ready?

The material should be dark brown in colour with a light, fragrant earthiness. The texture should be a good friable mixture that feels slightly moist yet crumbly to the touch. If the compost doesn't feel like this then it probably needs turning again and should be left for a few more weeks, or a bit longer. Exactly how long the composting process will take depends on a variety of factors, including outside temperature and weather conditions, as well as the constituent ingredients in your heap and the type of container you are using. But don't leave it for years and years, or the compost will decompose completely or wash away.

Where to place your compost system

There are a number of factors to consider when deciding where to site your compost equipment. Once you start filling it, you don't want to have to move it a few weeks or months later, so it's worth doing some initial planning before setting it up. Even in the smallest of outdoor gardens, a compost facility in the wrong place can look bad and become a frustration if it hasn't been considered as part of the overall design of a garden. Ease of access is also a big issue, as it should never be too difficult or discouraging to take waste to it.

Aesthetics

Open compost heaps are understandably considered by many to be an unsightly feature in the garden. Many people do not want to view a compost heap the moment they walk up the garden path or be looking at it from the patio when dining alfresco. So consider how it can be concealed, perhaps placed towards the back of the garden, or tucked away down the side of the house where it is not too obtrusive. Consider hedging or trellis for screening it if necessary.

However, don't forget that some of the closed compost systems can make good features in the garden, and can look great, so do consider giving it pride of place if you have a cool composting system.

Practicality

Although you may want the compost heap tucked out of sight, ideally it needs to be close by the house, with reasonable access and wide enough paths for a wheelbarrow. Otherwise the entire process of adding material to the compost becomes hard work. For example, if it is placed right at the top of a sloping garden, it will be time-consuming and frustrating if pushing a wheelbarrow, and the chances of regularly emptying out the kitchen waste caddy every few days becomes a less appealing option, particularly in the winter or when it's raining. So try to place the compost site as near as possible to the main garden area or house for ease of access.

If possible, ensure your compost heap isn't too far away to avoid long treks back and forth with the wheelbarrow.

Surfaces

Ideally the compost heap should be on bare soil to encourage microbes and worms to work their way into the compost and help the decomposition process. If you only have a patio, consider lifting a few slabs for the compost to sit directly onto the soil for maximum decomposition.

It is possible to place a compost heap on the lawn, but don't forget that the grass will die underneath after a short while. If there is no other option, the compost heap can be placed directly on a patio or concrete, and the one benefit of this is that it is easier to shovel up the decomposed compost from a hard surface. Avoid decking or timber as this will quickly rot underneath. It is recommended that if you put your compost heap directly onto a hard surface, a spadeful of soil should be added.

Sunshine and showers

Composts will rot faster if they receive a mix of sunshine and light shade, so are ideally placed in the dappled sunlight of a deciduous tree canopy, though this is not essential. If possible, place it on a level surface on well-drained soil. Although some moisture in the ground is beneficial for decomposition, you don't want the compost sitting in a puddle all year round.

Plant material such as nettles and comfrey can be added to water and left to rot to create a potent liquid compost feed.

LIQUID FEEDS
OR COMPOST 'TEAS'

Compost doesn't always come in solid form. There are liquid feeds, too, sometimes called compost 'teas', that can be used in the garden to reinvigorate plants and supply them with nutrients and minerals. Plants take liquid food into their systems quicker than nutrients from solid compost, so this can be a great instant 'tonic' for plants with yellowing foliage, wilting or just looking as if they are languishing and need a bit of immediate tender love and care.

The two most popular liquid feeds are comfrey and nettle. Both plants are easy to grow in the garden, and in fact grow so readily that they are considered as weeds by many gardeners. Bocking 14 is a popular comfrey variety and, if room allows, it is worth considering planting up a small area with some of these plants for a regular supply of their leaves to transform into a rich liquid feed.

The plants can be propagated by division and planted at a spacing of about 15cm (6in) between plants. Cut them back every few weeks during the growing season to add to a liquid feed and they will rapidly regrow ready for harvesting again soon afterwards.

Nettle or comfrey?

As a general rule, nettles are rich in nitrogen and therefore the liquid feed is ideal for getting young plants underway and growing vigorously, promoting lots of foliage and growth. Comfrey is high in potassium, which is useful for developing fruit flavour and flower colour, so plants benefit from this feed slightly later on in the season, from the early stages of flowering through to the ripening of fruits or vegetables. Many gardeners will use both feeds and alternate them weekly to ensure they're getting a balanced diet of both nitrogen and potassium.

The Bocking 14 comfrey variety is rich in potassium and makes a superb liquid feed to give to plants when they're flowering or fruiting.

Making liquid feed

To make liquid feed, cut back the foliage of nettles or comfrey. Chop them up into small pieces and fill up a bucket. Pour water into the bucket up to the top. It may be necessary to place a brick on the foliage to prevent it from floating on the top. Place the bucket somewhere out of the way as this liquid feed can really smell when the foliage starts to decompose in the water.

After about a month the liquid will be ready to use. Strain off the foliage and store the concentrated liquid in recycled bottles. When you wish to use the feed, mix it in a watering can using 10 parts water to 1 part liquid comfrey/nettle concentrate. Water the soil around the base of the plants with the liquid every week during the growing season.

Perennial-weed liquid feed

As a rule perennial weeds should never be added to the compost heap, as they quickly spread if their roots are given an opportunity to take hold. However, there is one exception, and this is after the plants have been 'drowned' in a bucket. Use a brick or stone to hold the plants under the water and put a lid on top to exclude sunlight. The liquid can then be strained and used as a liquid feed concentrate (dilute like nettle or comfrey feed; see above), while the sludgy remainder of the plant in the bottom of the bucket can then be added to the compost heap without fear of it spreading. It can take between two months and a year of 'drowning' the weeds before they can safely be used on the compost heap. You can tell when they are dead, as the plant material, including the roots, will be mushy and no longer solid.

Instead of using a shredder to chop up leaves to make leaf mould, simply drive over the leaves with a rotary mower.

MOWING UP LEAVES
FOR LEAF MOULD

Fallen leaves can be collected up and made into a type of compost known as leaf mould. Some leaves can take longer than others to break down. The leaves of some deciduous trees, such as oak and beech, are coarse, thick and high in tannins, and decompose slowly, meaning they can take months to rot. Thinner leaves from trees like acers, limes and elder are much lighter and break down faster.

However, all leaves will break down more quickly when they are broken up into smaller fragments. There are numerous ways of chopping up fallen leaves to make leaf mould, the most obvious method being putting them through a garden shredder.

Leaves can be shredded just as effectively using a rotary mower, as described opposite. And it saves having to pick all the leaves up.

Top tips for making your own leaf mould:

- Rake the leaves out into rows over a part of a lawn.
- Ensure the blades of the mower are lifted onto a high setting.
- Fit the grass collection box onto the back.
- Drive slowly over the leaves.
- Turn off the mower and remove the collection box.
- Add the finely chopped leaves to the compost heap or create a separate pile of leaf mould.

If you have less space, tip the shredded leaves into old compost bags or sacks, add a splash of water to speed up the decomposition, and leave them in a hidden, tucked-away, shady corner of the garden until they have decomposed into a lovely, dark brown crumbly cake. The process should take about a year.

A wire-tined rake is ideal for removing leaves from the lawn to make into leaf mould.

GREEN MANURES

If you really have no inclination for a compost bin or heap but do have soil to improve, it is still possible to add extra fertility and condition by sowing a green manure wherever you have bare ground or free space. Green manures are specific plants that are sown, grow fast and then cut down and turned into the soil, where the natural micro-organisms will compost them in situ. Like composting in a container, it is really only a more controlled, slightly quicker version of nature's waste cycle. Green manure plants are chosen for their speed of growth as well as their fertility benefits. There are green manures, such as winter tares and rye, that will slowly grow through the winter months to be chopped down a couple of weeks before spring planting. Other manures, from the pea and bean family, will add nitrogen to the soil when they have decomposed. Fast-growing plants such as phacelia and fenugreek planted in spring and summer, can also help keep down other weeds as well as adding to soil fertility. All have the added benefit of preventing soil erosion. Although they are mostly used by vegetable gardeners, they could work just as well in the ornamental garden, or even sown in pots.

Wormeries take up hardly any space and can be used to make both liquid and solid compost material for the garden.

WORMERIES

Composting using worms, known as vermicomposting, is fascinating and really quite rewarding as it produces both a liquid feed loved by plants and a superb, nutrient-rich compost that gardeners often refer to as 'black gold'.

Although it is possible to make your own worm bin, there are any number of ready-made worm bins or 'wormeries' available to buy. The best have at least two compartments, a lower one to collect liquid, which can be siphoned off and diluted as a liquid feed, and a composting compartment above where worms convert waste into compost.

Compost worms are different from the earthworms found in garden soil and are known by various names – brandling, red wigglers, tiger or manure worms – but the different species are all specialists in living and eating decaying natural matter. If you already have a compost heap in the garden you may recognise them and be able to start your wormery off by picking some out. If not you can buy packs of live compost worms from suppliers.

There are some simple rules to remember to get the best out of your wormery. The worms are most active in warm, moist conditions and will stop recycling your waste in extreme temperatures, so make sure your wormery is sheltered and not exposed to extremes of heat and cold. A well-ventilated site is also essential, and too much acidity and liquid will be harmful. Be careful when you add watery or acidic waste such as lettuce and citrus.

Wormeries work most efficiently if small amounts of chopped-up waste are added every few days. Waste you can add includes cooked and raw vegetable matter, teabags and coffee grounds, fruit, small amounts of non-glossy paper, cardboard and bread, green weeds and leaves. Avoid dairy products, meat and fish, which may quickly create a fly and odour problem, and woody material, as the worms will have difficulty processing this quickly.

Problems with your wormery such as bad odours are usually the result of neglect, but are easily remedied with a bit of common-sense maintenance and experience.

It is also possible to apply the same principles to composting using snails rather than worms, although most gardeners would find it difficult to accept such a conglomeration of molluscs in one place; see page 94 for more information.

Making your own basic wormery

If you have basic DIY skills and access to a few tools, making your own wormery is a much cheaper option than buying a ready-made kit and is surprisingly easy to do.

Worms will be happy in any home that meets their basic life needs. Air and moisture are vital; darkness and reasonable temperatures, neither too hot nor too cold, are also required. Effectively, all sorts of plastic or wood boxes will do the job with just a few minor adjustments.

The simplest type of wormery can be made using just one container with a lid.

You will need:
- A box with a lid, approximately 65cm (26in) long, 30cm (12in) wide and 30cm (12in) deep. Anything that does not let light in will do
- Bricks to stand it on
- Newspaper or cardboard
- Worm bedding (this can be compost from your compost bin mixed with cardboard and soil, or worm compost from someone who already has a wormery)
- Composting worms (you can buy them or collect 300–500 from another wormery, with permission of course). Do not collect earthworms
- A drill

Method:

- Drill plenty of holes in the bottom of your box to ensure a good airflow. A 12.5mm (½in) drill bit is perfect for the job.
- Drill smaller air holes just under the top lid and in the lid itself if it is to be placed in a sheltered, protected area. Plenty of air is important, but you need to be careful to prevent too much rain and light getting in.
- Place the box on bricks or blocks of wood or plastic to keep the base off the ground. This way you ensure a good airflow and prevent flooding in heavy rain. Ideally, place your wormery in a sheltered spot where it can be protected from extremes of heat and cold.
- Cover the bottom of the box with a sheet of newspaper or cardboard to stop the worms falling out. As long as they are fed and happy in their environment they will not determinedly try to escape, so this should be more than adequate.
- Add half a bucket of worm bedding. You can buy this from specialist suppliers, but old compost, or worm compost from another source, will be fine.
- Add your worms. About 300 will be fine for a standard storage box as they will quickly reproduce in good conditions.
- Add a small amount of organic waste, such as kitchen vegetable peelings, fruit and scraps of cooked food.
- Cover with a piece of cardboard or newspaper to keep the environment moist and dark, and put the lid on.

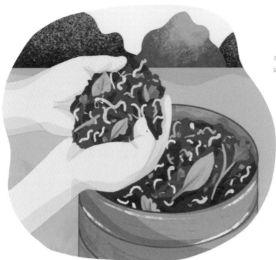

It is possible to buy bespoke wormeries, but it is very easy to build your own too.

- Keep adding small amounts of chopped-up food on a regular basis, rather than adding large quantities all at once, and avoid adding too much citrus, onion and spices, as worms are sensitive to acidity and strong flavours. Check regularly to see how much your worms can actually eat and adjust accordingly, or you may end up with a pile of rotting, smelly, uneaten food.
- Add small amounts of shredded cardboard or paper on a regular basis to ensure good airflow and moisture control.
- If you want to collect worm juice you can leave a tray underneath to catch any drips, and use it diluted 10 parts water to 1 part liquid as a supercharged liquid feed for your plants.

Making a bigger, better wormery

If you are confident in your DIY skills you could consider making a bigger, better wormery, using three containers. This way you can easily harvest both compost and worm juice without disturbing your worm population too much.

You will need:

- Three containers (the same size as the ones used in the basic wormery on page 89), one with a lid
- A water butt tap
- Bricks to stand your wormery on, high enough to be able to use the tap, plus more bricks as spacers inside
- Split pins
- Pieces of fine-gauge mesh (6mm [¼in]) to fit the bottoms of the containers.

Tips for the perfect wormery

- Position your wormery where it is protected from extremes of temperature. If possible, 10–26°C (50–79°F) is ideal.
- Cut up food waste and cardboard as small as possible to make it easier for worms to digest.
- Avoid adding too much grease and smelly waste, or any animal products. These are more difficult to digest and the smell may linger, or be avoided completely by the worms.
- Gnats and flies can become a problem, especially if the mixture is too moist. Leave the lid off to dry out the bin contents or add more small pieces of cardboard to soak up the excess.

Method:

- Drill a line of small air holes around each of the three boxes towards their top lip for aeration.
- Drill a hole in one box towards the bottom and install the water butt tap. The bottom box will collect any worm juice produced, which can be decanted through the tap and diluted to make liquid food. Remember to drain it off regularly.
- To stop the worms drowning, place a couple of bricks in the bottom and fit a piece of mesh on top to create a collection area for liquid.
- For the worm boxes, cut out large holes in the base with a jigsaw then cover the base with a piece of mesh, ideally held in place with split pins (you will need to drill 4mm/$^1/_6$ in holes in the box to fit these).
- Add newspaper, worm bedding, worms and a small amount of kitchen waste to one of the two boxes (following the instructions above), then stack on top of the base collecting box.
- When this is full you can begin to fill the top box with organic matter and your worms will migrate upwards in their search for new food. The fully composted box can then be removed and the compost harvested before being refilled. Having two boxes means that you do not have to pick out your worms each time you want to use your compost.
- Place your completed wormery outside in a sheltered spot, on bricks or something similar so that the tap is accessible.

Snaileries

For most gardeners, snails are the enemy. There are, however, a brave few who are happy to harness the snail's voracious appetite for plant material to their own advantage, perhaps accepting the maxim that you should keep your friends close but your enemies closer. A snailery is traditionally used to farm snails for human consumption, but can also, with minor changes, become a compost factory.

To make a snailery, you'll need a container with plenty of ventilation, such as an old mesh laundry basket, but you'll also need to add a snail-proof lid. The container should be placed over a flat container filled with water, which acts as a sort of moat to prevent escape. Leftover lettuce or cabbage peelings and waste vegetables are fed to the snails inside, who rapidly munch the plant material and excrete it as nutrient-rich droppings, which can be added as a mulch to plants in the garden or diluted to make liquid feed. The snails may also need to be given a dish of water in dry weather.

The advantage of this kind of composting is that it gives you somewhere to rehome and reuse any snails you find elsewhere in the garden, especially if you are squeamish. However, you may feel that increasing your garden's snail population, and the risk of an entire colony of snails escaping, outweigh the value of the compost produced, although *escargots* could become a suppertime favourite!

TOP 10 TIPS FOR PERFECT COMPOST

1. Regularly turn your compost.
2. Use a mix of green and brown material.
3. Chop up larger material.
4. Avoid perennial weeds.
5. Ensure your compost bin is rodent-proof.
6. Have more than one compost bin.
7. Prevent compost from drying out.
8. Place bin so it has good access from the house.
9. Place bin directly on soil if possible.
10. Try wormeries (see page 87) if you don't have room for a compost bin.

INDEX